Hitler's Rise
to Power
and the Holocaust

Titles in The Holocaust in History Series

—The Holocaust in History—

Hitler's Rise to Power and the Holocaust

Linda Jacobs Altman

Enslow Publishers, Inc.

40 Industrial Road   PO Box 38
Box 398   Aldershot
Berkeley Heights, NJ 07922 Hants GU12 6BP
USA   UK

http://www.enslow.com

Library of Congress Cataloging-in-Publication Data

Altman, Linda Jacobs, 1943-
    Hitler's rise to power and the Holocaust / Linda Jacobs Altman.
        p. cm. — (The Holocaust in history)
    Includes bibliographical references and index.
    Summary: Explores events in Germany that led up to World War II including
Hitler's rise to power and the creation of the Third Reich.
    ISBN 0-7660-1991-8
        1. Hitler, Adolf, 1889-1945—Juvenile literature. 2. Heads of state—
Germany—Biography—Juvenile literature. 3. National socialism—Juvenile
literature. 4. Germany—History—1933-1945— Juvenile literature. 5. Holocaust,
Jewish (1939-1945)—Juvenile literature. [1. Hitler, Adolf, 1889-1945. 2. Heads of
state—Germany. 3. National socialism. 4. Germany—History—1933-1945.
5. Holocaust, Jewish (1939-1945)] I. Title. II. Series.
DD247.H5 A8124   2003
943.086'092—dc21
                                                            2002151083

Printed in the United States of America

10 9 8 7 6 5 4 3 2 1

To Our Readers: We have done our best to make sure all Internet Addresses in this
book were active and appropriate when we went to press. However, the author and
the publisher have no control over and assume no liability for the material avail-
able on those Internet sites or on other Web sites they may link to. Any comments
or suggestions can be sent by e-mail to comments@enslow.com or to the address
on the back cover.

Illustration Credits: AP/Wide World Photos, p. 69; Bud Tullin, courtesy of
USHMM Photo Archives, p. 60; Bundesarchiv, courtesy of USHMM Photo
Archives, p. 5; courtesy of USHMM Photo Archives, pp. 2, 48, 53, 54, 61,
63, 67, 78, 80, 90; Enslow Publishers, Inc., pp. 9, 91; Harry S. Truman
Library, courtesy of USHMM Photo Archives, pp. 37, 65; James Sanders,
courtesy of USHMM Photo Archives, pp. 23, 26; Library of Congress, pp.
10, 17, 33, 41, 43; Library of Congress, courtesy of USHMM Photo
Archives, p. 46; Muzej Revolucije Narodnosti Jugoslavije, courtesy of
USHMM Photo Archives, p. 29; National Archives, pp. 6, 12, 13, 19, 24,
31, 40, 55, 72, 87, 89; National Archives, courtesy of USHMM Photo
Archives, pp. 21, 35, 77, 81; National Museum of American Jewish
History, courtesy of USHMM Photo Archives, p. 11; Richard Freimark,
courtesy of USHMM Photo Archives, p. 1, 3, 51; Robert A. Schmuhl,
courtesy of USHMM Photo Archives, p. 83; Stadtarchiv Mittweida,
courtesy of USHMM Photo Archives, pp. 57, 74.

Cover Illustration: Courtesy of USHMM Photo Archives

Contents

German troops bombed the Polish capital of Warsaw in
September, 1939.

Introduction
World War II and
the Holocaust

On September 1, 1939, German troops invaded Poland. Two days later, Britain and France declared war on Germany. World War II had begun. Under Adolf Hitler and his National Socialist German Workers' Party, also called the Nazi party, Germany would soon conquer most of Europe.

Hitler planned to build a *Reich*, or empire, that would last for a thousand years. He believed that Northern Europeans, or Aryans as he called them, were a master race—a group of people superior to others.

Hitler falsely believed that some people were inferior, such as Jews, Gypsies, Poles, Russians, and people of color. These people would be given no rights in his Reich. Some would be exterminated, or killed. Others would be kept alive only so long as they served their Aryan masters. It was a dark and terrible vision that cost millions of lives.

In the early days of the war, Germany seemed unbeatable. One nation after another fell to the German *blitzkrieg*, or "lightning war." The Nazis conquered Poland in just twenty-six days. Denmark, Norway, Belgium, the Netherlands, and France fell in the spring of 1940.

By the end of 1940, the Germans had occupied most of Western Europe and made alliances with Italy and Japan. The Axis, as this alliance was called, soon conquered parts of Asia, Eastern Europe, and North Africa.

In 1941, the picture changed. In June, Germany invaded the Soviet Union, now called Russia. America entered the war on December 7, when Japan attacked the United States naval base in Pearl Harbor, Hawaii. The Germans soon found themselves fighting the British and the Americans in the West, and the Soviets in the East. They also devoted men and resources to exterminating Jews and other people the Nazis saw as inferior.

Even when the war turned against Germany, this slaughter did not stop. Trains that could have carried troops and supplies to the fighting fronts were used instead to transport victims to death camps. The killing continued until the last possible moment.

After Germany surrendered on May 7, 1945, survivors began telling what they had suffered. Pictures of starving prisoners, mass graves, and gas chambers disguised as showers appeared in newspapers and movie newsreels. People all over the world were horrified.

By the end of 1940, the Germans had occupied most of Western Europe, including Poland, Luxembourg, Denmark, Norway, France, Belgium, and the Netherlands.

As survivors told their stories, the horror grew. New words came into the language. Old words took on new meanings. Holocaust came to represent mass murder on a scale that had never been seen before. Genocide described the systematic killing of specific racial or ethnic groups.

These words are reminders of a grim truth—human beings can do terrible things

The United States entered World War II on December 7, 1941, when Japan attacked the Pearl Harbor naval base.

In Germany, trains were used to transport people to death camps rather than to bring supplies to the troops.

to one another. This is why knowing about the Holocaust is so important. Knowledge is the best defense against the hatred that produced the Nazi racial state and caused the death of innocent millions.

The German emperor, Kaiser Wilhelm II (center), abandoned his throne near the end of World War I.

1

Beginnings

The story of World War II and the Holocaust does not begin with the first shots fired in 1939. It begins with the end of World War I on November 11, 1918. On that day, Germany surrendered to the Allied nations who had fought against it. The Allies were led by England, France, and the United States.

Near the end of World War I, the German *kaiser*, or emperor, had abandoned his throne. A new, democratic government took his place—a government elected by the people. The leaders of that government signed the armistice, or cease-fire, that stopped the fighting.

The German people were stunned. The military had been telling them that victory was close at hand. No enemy troops had invaded German soil or attacked German cities. To have lost was unthinkable. Many people called it a stab in the back. They believed that the new democratic government had betrayed the nation.

Old Fears and New Directions

In January 1919, Allied leaders gathered at Versailles, France. Their job was to create a permanent peace treaty. After a long and bloody war, many of these people wanted to punish the Germans. The treaty they signed on June 28, 1919, was called the Treaty of Versailles.

This treaty stripped Germany of some of its territory and cut the size of its army. It made the German government pay over thirty billion dollars in damages to the Allies and accept all responsibility for starting the war.

Public reaction in Germany was swift. A popular newspaper expressed the feelings of many Germans when it demanded "vengeance for the shame of 1919."[1]

German democracy could not have begun under worse circumstances. Germans were used to an authoritarian government run by emperors and aristocrats. Many Germans feared democracy. They also feared the communism of the newly-formed government in Russia. This government grew out of the

Russian Revolution of 1917 and eventually became the Union of Soviet Socialist Republics (USSR), or Soviet Union.

Under communism in the Soviet Union, everything would belong to "the people" and be controlled by the government. Communism abolished private property and private enterprise.

To spread their form of government, the communists called for worldwide revolution. In postwar Germany, many people were willing to listen. There was unrest in the nation, especially among war veterans. Not only had they been defeated in battle, many of them were out of work. They made a good audience for communist ideas.

Knowing this, the German army formed a special unit to investigate groups and people suspected of communist beliefs. One of the men chosen for that unit was Adolf Hitler.

Hitler the "Artist"

The man who would one day rule Germany was Austrian by birth. He was born on April 20, 1889, to Alois Hitler and his third wife, Klara. A mystery surrounding this family would embarrass the adult Adolf Hitler.

Adolf's father, Alois, was born to an unmarried maid named Maria Schickelgruber. The identity of Alois's father is uncertain.

But most likely it was Johann Heidler, the man Maria married when her son was five years old. When Alois became an adult, he took his father's name. However, he changed the spelling from "Heidler" to "Hitler."

If Alois Hitler had not changed his name, his son would have become "Adolf Schickelgruber." Hitler's enemies often made fun of this possibility. As one Hitler biographer noted, "It is difficult to imagine seventy million Germans shouting in all seriousness, 'Heil Schickelgruber!'"[2]

Adolf Hitler had a difficult childhood. His father was demanding and critical. He expected his son to follow in his footsteps and work for the Austrian government. The young Hitler had bigger things in mind. First he wanted to be an artist. Then he wanted to be an architect. He failed at both.

Instead, he found himself drifting and alone in Vienna. Rather than take a regular job, he lived from hand to mouth. He sometimes stayed in what would be called a homeless shelter today. To make money, he drew picture postcards and sold them on the streets.

Hitler came to hate Vienna. For him, it was a place of failure and poverty. Later in his life, he would recall how "foreign" the city had seemed to him: "I was repelled . . . by this whole mixture of [people:] Czechs, Poles,

Adolf Hitler's father, Alois Hitler.

Hungarians, Ruthenians, Serbs, and Croats, and everywhere . . . Jews and more Jews."[3] In the spring of 1912, Hitler left Austria and moved to Munich, Germany.

Hitler the Soldier

Hitler was still in Munich two years later when Germany went to war. He quickly enlisted in the German army and marched off to fight for the Fatherland—the name Germans often used for their country. Though he never rose above the rank of corporal, Hitler found a place for himself in the army. In civilian life, he had been a shabby, failed artist with few friends and no social life. In the army he became somebody, at least in his own eyes.

The war gave Hitler an outlet for his fanatical German nationalism, or devotion to one's country. Hitler believed in *"Deutschland ueber Alles,"* or "Germany over all." He believed that Germany should rule the world.

When Germany surrendered in 1918, Hitler's world fell apart. Defeat had been unthinkable. Only some dark and evil plot could explain it.

Looking for someone to blame, Hitler settled on Jews, Communists, and the new democratic government. Like other right-wing extremists in Germany, he concluded that a stab in the

When Germany went to war, Hitler enlisted in the German army and fought in World War I.

back from these traitors led to his country's defeat. This was not true, but for Hitler it was very real. In his rage, he decided to fight back by going into politics.

Hitler the Investigator

Hitler's road to political life began when the army recruited him to investigate radical, or extreme, political groups. During training for this work, he discovered his talent for public speaking.

One of Hitler's instructors later recalled watching him speak to a group of his fellow trainees:

> The men seemed spellbound by one of their number who was [talking] in a strange, guttural [rough and hoarse] voice. . . . I saw a pale, small face, under an unsoldierly flowing lock of hair, with close-cropped mustache, and . . . large light blue eyes that shone fanatically.[4]

Hitler's speaking ability soon attracted more attention. One of his first assignments was to investigate a tiny political group called the German Workers' Party. On September 12, 1919, Hitler went to a party meeting of about twenty-five people in a Munich beer hall.

Hitler had only come to observe, but he couldn't resist speaking out. He shared his thoughts on German nationalism and pride. When he had finished, the audience was silent. Party founder Anton Drexler was wide-eyed with admiration. He personally asked Hitler to return.

A few days later, Hitler received a postcard from the German Workers' Party. It said that he had been accepted as a party member. He was being invited to a meeting of the party leaders.

At first, Hitler did not know what to think. The party was little more than a debate group for people who didn't fit in elsewhere. Still,

Hitler had a talent for public speaking. The crowd listening to him was usually captivated by his words.

there could be advantages to joining an unknown and poorly-organized group. Hitler realized that "it was only in a Party which, like himself, was beginning at the bottom that he had any prospect of playing a leading part and imposing his ideas. In the established Parties . . . he would be a nobody."[5]

Once Hitler joined the German Workers' Party, he threw himself into the work. To him, the party was like modeling clay that he could shape and mold to his liking. It became his platform for launching a career that would turn hatred into national policy, a guiding principle for the country.

The Growth of National Socialism

Hitler wasted no time in molding the German Workers' Party to his own liking. He soon convinced the committee of party leaders to organize larger meetings. He sent invitations, put up flyers, and placed advertisements in nationalist and anti-Semitic newspapers.

As the crowds grew, so did Hitler's ambition. After only three months, he called for total reform of the party.

The Propaganda Chief

Party founder Anton Drexler was a plodding man with no talent for speaking or persuading people. He could, however, recognize these qualities in others. He saw them clearly in Adolf Hitler.

Ernst Röhm was the organizer of the dreaded SA.

With Drexler's support, Hitler rose quickly in the German Workers' Party. In January, 1920, he became chief of propaganda. His job was to spread the party's message. Hitler also worked with Drexler to write a party platform, or statement of goals and beliefs. It included removing Jews from government and newspaper jobs, renouncing the Treaty of Versailles, and creating a powerful government to control the life of the nation.

Hitler presented this platform at a party rally on February 24, 1920. Over two thousand people attended. Some came to see what the fuss was all about, some came to cheer, and some even came to heckle.

Hitler had a plan for the hecklers. A squad, or small group, of his army friends went through the crowd with billy clubs and whips, clearing protestors from the hall. This security squad became the foundation for the dreaded Stormtroops, or *Sturmabteilung* (SA).

Stormtroops and Swastikas

The SA was organized by Ernst Röhm, a war veteran who was one of the earliest members of the party. Röhm was a battle-scarred bull of a man, ready to work with anyone who promised to make Germany strong again. Röhm believed he had found such a man in Hitler. Beyond that, he did not ask questions.

Hitler designed the Nazi party's flag. It had a red background with a swastika inside a white circle.

Röhm's Stormtroops were street-fighters, always ready to crack heads, fight with rival groups, or terrorize anyone who criticized the party. They were often called Brownshirts because of the color of their uniforms. With their whips, clubs, and guns, they gave an image of toughness to the little party with the big ideas.

Hitler worked to strengthen that image. It was his idea to change the party name from the German Workers' Party to something more impressive: the National Socialist German Worker's (Nazi) Party. Nazi is an abbreviation of the first part of the German name: *Nationalsozialistische.*

Hitler also designed the party's flag, which would become a symbol of death and oppression to millions. He chose a red background with a black hooked "x", or swastika, inside a white circle. Soon, swastikas appeared everywhere at Nazi functions. They were on posters, banners, and flags. Swastika armbands decorated the khaki uniforms of the Stormtroops.

The Meaning of Fascism

Behind the banners, uniforms, and rallies, was a political philosophy called fascism. Fascism was the foundation of the Nazi party. The word comes from the name of an ancient

Roman symbol of official authority. The fasces was a bundle of rods tied around two raised axe heads. The rods stood for punishment, the axe heads for execution. It was first used in 1919 to describe a political movement led by Benito Mussolini in Italy.

It is difficult to define fascism. When Mussolini was asked for his definition, he simply replied, "It is action."[1] He did not like to be pinned down to a detailed ideology, or system of beliefs.

Hitler shared this attitude. Though he helped to write the Nazi platform, he did not feel bound by it. The party he wanted to build would not be based upon political philosophy. It would be held together by his leadership.

A fascist leader is an absolute dictator whose word is law. Under his control, the State is not simply the nation's government. It is a total way of life. The State tells people how to behave, what to believe, and where to live and work. It even tells people how to raise and educate their children.

The idea of a constant struggle is important to fascism. Among other things, fascists believe that constant struggle eliminates the weak and purifies the strong. In a fascist society, only the strong have a right to survive. This belief in the "survival of the fittest" makes fascist regimes brutal and warlike.

Benito Mussolini, left, shown here with Hitler, was the leader of the fascist movement in Italy.

They are also fiercely nationalistic, or patriotic to an extreme. Fascists prefer conquest of other nations rather than cooperation. They fear any form of foreign influence.

In Nazi fascism, only Germany mattered. Ernst Röhm expressed this attitude clearly in his autobiography: "I approve of whatever serves the purpose of German freedom. I oppose whatever runs counter to it. Europe, [yes], the whole world, may go down in flames—what concern is it of ours? Germany must live and be free."[2]

Hitler Takes Over

This extreme nationalism appealed to the party leaders. Most of them agreed with the party platform outlined by Drexler and Hitler. Not all of them, however, liked Hitler as well as they liked his ideas. Many had become tired of his lectures and the tactics he used to get his way.

When a committee within the party tried to limit his growing power, Hitler moved swiftly to stop them. The way he handled the situation was masterful. It showed the sly cleverness that would serve him well in his rise to power. Instead of arguing his case, he simply offered to quit the party.

The committee could not afford to lose Hitler. He was their best speaker and organizer.

Röhm, like other Nazis, believed that only Germany mattered. German freedom was the ultimate goal.

Without him, they would be back in dingy meeting rooms, doomed to insignificance.

When the committee refused to accept his resignation, Hitler knew he had the upper hand. He was quick to use it. He demanded total control of the party. There would be no more committee, no more bickering over details. There would only be his word, and his word would be law. After some frantic maneuvering on both sides, Adolf Hitler stood alone at the top of the Nazi party.

According to one journalist, Hitler's victory "established the 'leadership principle' which was to be the law first of the Nazi party and then of the Third Reich. The 'Fuehrer' had arrived on the German scene."[3]

A Company of Conspirators

As *Führer* (leader) of the party, Hitler surrounded himself with loyal followers. Of the original party leaders, only Ernst Röhm kept a place of importance. Hitler felt a soldier's bond with Röhm. Both men had served in combat and shed blood for Germany.

Röhm's taste for violence served Hitler's purposes during the early days of his rise to power. Röhm's brute squad, the Stormtroops, could always be counted on to keep order at meetings and rallies. Their presence was enough to silence most protest.

Hitler demanded total control of the Nazi party.

The rest of Hitler's inner circle was filled with men who idolized him. He did not want to surround himself with independent thinkers. He wanted people who would follow him blindly, yet were smart enough to know how to carry out his orders.

Early members of the inner circle included Rudolf Hess, Hermann Göring, and Heinrich Himmler. Each would later play a leading role in the Third Reich. Each was a social misfit who shared Hitler's prejudices and hatreds. Each in his own way regarded the Führer with almost religious devotion.

Hitler's Henchmen

The shy, hero-worshiping Hess was perhaps the most dedicated follower of all. As Hitler's personal aide he was always at the Führer's side. For Hess, this was enough. He did not crave power for himself. He was a born follower, content to live in Hitler's shadow and to obey every order.

Hermann Göring was far more ambitious. He was a decorated war veteran who shared Hitler's horror of the Treaty of Versailles. Raised among the aristocracy, or nobility, and trained in a military academy, Göring saw himself as a German hero. Peacetime had left him at loose ends. Göring found the cause he needed in the Nazi party.

Rudolf Hess would play a major role in the Third Reich. He was one of Hitler's most dedicated followers. This photo was taken while Hess was in prison during the trials following the war.

Göring served in several different jobs. He was head of the SA for a time, and later became commander of the *Luftwaffe* (the German air force). Medals, awards, and impressive job titles fed his sense of self-importance.

Göring liked to think of himself as a man of action. He was not interested in the party's philosophy, or beliefs. He once said that he "joined the party because I was a revolutionary, not because of any ideological nonsense."[4]

Ideology, another word for beliefs, did interest Heinrich Himmler. A chicken farmer by trade, Himmler considered himself a mystic, a person interested in mysteries of life. He dabbled in astrology and other occult, or secret, practices. For him, belief in the German Master Race was practically a religion.

Many people found Himmler the most frightening of all the Nazi leaders. With his round, soft face and poor eyesight, he appeared to be the mildest of men. He did not rant like Hitler or strut like Göring. Yet he could unleash terror and mass murder without a pang of conscience.

He became chief of Hitler's dreaded *Shutzstaffel*, or SS. This powerful organization combined security police and intelligence-gathering functions. Under Himmler's leadership, the SS would make Germany into

Hermann Göring served in several different positions within the Nazi party. He was an ambitious and decorated war veteran who saw himself as a hero.

a police state and be responsible for carrying out the Holocaust. As chief of the SS, Himmler could transform his darkest fantasies into even darker realities. He once called upon his troops to

> be honest, decent, loyal and comradely to members of our own blood and to no one else. What happens to the Russians, what happens to the Czechs, is a matter of utter indifference to me. . . . Whether the other peoples live in comfort or perish of hunger interests me only in so far as we need them as slaves for our culture; apart from that it does not interest me.[5]

Hitler thoroughly approved of this harsh racism. For him, it was the heart and soul of Nazi ideology. He could not imagine that his Thousand-Year Reich would include Jews, people of color, or Slavs such as Poles and Russians. His empire would belong to a race of Aryan supermen. It would create *lebensraum*, or living space, for them by conquering vast territories in Eastern Europe and Russia.

"Nature has not reserved this soil for the future possession of any particular nation or race," Hitler once wrote. "On the contrary, this soil exists for the people which possesses the force to take it."[6]

In Hitler's plan, Jews would be eliminated. Both communism and democracy would be destroyed. In their place would be an all-powerful State, and a leader who could not be challenged or questioned by anyone. Hitler himself would be that leader for as long as he lived.

When Hitler first spoke of these things, few Germans took him seriously. He was just a "crackpot" with strange ideas and a handful of deeply disturbed followers. Not until the fall of 1923 did people begin to realize how far this "crackpot" would go to achieve his goals.

A Failed Revolution

Adolf Hitler was not a patient man. Rallies and speeches would only go so far in building the Nazi party. Despite his best efforts, real power seemed far away. Hitler needed a bold and dramatic event, something that would seem heroic. He decided to stage a putsch, or revolt, against the Bavarian state government.

The idea was to capture government leaders and force them to surrender. Nazis would then seize the capital in Munich and transform the section of Germany known as "Bavaria" into a National Socialist state. Bavaria would then become a power base for spreading National Socialism throughout Germany.

The Beer Hall Putsch

Hitler was not the sort of man to bother with details. He often acted on impulse, without thinking his actions through. This led to mistakes. He would push too hard, then be surprised when things did not turn out the way he expected. This happened with the Beer Hall Putsch.

On the night of November 8, 1923, Hitler burst into a Munich beer hall, where an important political meeting was in progress. Hess and Göring marched at Hitler's side.

During the beer hall putsch, the Stormtroops sealed the room's exits.

Ernst Röhm and his Stormtroops sealed the exits.

Hitler fired his gun into the air. Shouting over the sudden confusion, he announced the revolution. Then he herded Bavaria's three most important leaders into a back room. He threatened to shoot them if they did not give in to his demands.

The men held their ground. Hitler tried more threats, then persuasion. Nobody budged. He boasted that the war hero General Erich Ludendorff had agreed to command the armed forces of his new government.

Actually, Ludendorff had agreed to no such thing. He did not even know about the putsch. One of Hitler's men simply showed up at his doorway and asked him to come to the beer hall.

When Ludendorff arrived, he was furious. He greeted the upstart corporal with a cold-eyed stare. But he did not leave. For reasons of his own, he decided to go along with the idea. Under his influence, the three officials seemed to agree as well. Hitler was over-joyed. One observer noted that he "had a childlike, frank expression of happiness that I shall never forget."[1]

Hitler's happiness did not last for long. Later that night, the officials withdrew their support. None of them had joined the Nazis

Ludendorff did not know about the beer hall putsch before he arrived on the scene, but he decided to go along with Hitler anyway.

willingly, they said. They had been forced into making false statements.

Hitler was stunned. He was also furious. This reversal of fortune had caught him by surprise. Ludendorff suggested a simple, straightforward plan. He and Hitler, with all their followers, would march into the heart of the city and take over the War Ministry.

So it was that a legendary general and a former corporal led some three thousand Nazis into a battle they could not possibly win. The would-be revolutionaries never reached their goal. The police blocked their way.

There was an exchange of words, followed by an exchange of bullets that lasted only a minute. History does not record who fired the first shot. Sixteen Nazis and three police-men were killed. Many more people were wounded. The putsch came to a less than glo-rious end.

Hitler on Trial

Hitler and the Nazis appeared to be finished as a political force. Not only had they failed at their "revolution," they had looked foolish doing it. Under fire, Stormtroopers lost their swagger and scattered like frightened chil-dren. Hitler himself had run at the first sign of trouble. He took refuge in the home of friends, where he was arrested two days later.

If Hitler found his own behavior embarrassing or shameful, he gave no sign of it. In court, he relied on his famous speaking skills. He spoke well in his own defense, and people listened. In the end, the trial made Hitler into a national figure.

Some scoffed at him and his disorganized revolution. Others saw him, however misguided, as a patriot and hero. Even the judges were impressed. Many people were also sympathetic to his right-wing nationalism. They shared his dislike for the democratic constitution "forced" upon Germany after its defeat in World War I.

The judges could have sentenced Hitler to life in prison for high treason, or betraying the German nation. Instead, they sentenced him to five years. The other Nazi defendants also drew short prison terms, while General Ludendorff was found not guilty.

Hitler was sent to Landsberg Fortress, an old castle converted into a prison. Life at Landsberg was far from harsh. Hitler and his fellow revolutionaries had rooms instead of cells and were free to move about the prison's public areas.

While in prison, Hitler wrote his book, *Mein Kampf (My Struggle)*. It was part autobiography, part political statement. It also

Hitler wrote the book *Mein Kampf* while he was in prison. In it, he expressed many racist ideas.

served as a platform for Hitler's racist ideas. Rudolf Hess, imprisoned along with Hitler, helped edit, revise, and organize the material in *Mein Kampf.*

On December 20, 1924, Hitler was released from Landsberg, after serving less than a year of his sentence. He went into seclusion, staying with the family that had sheltered him after the failed putsch. Eventually, he started the long and difficult process of rebuilding the party.

It was not an easy job. After the putsch, the Bavarian government had outlawed the Nazi party. Some members went underground to keep it alive. Others formed organizations with new names so they could continue to play a public role.

The New National Socialism

Ernst Röhm replaced his banned Stormtroops with a new private army called the *Frontbann,* or "Rulers of the Front." By the spring of 1925, he had mobilized over thirty thousand men.

Other Nazi party members formed a political organization called the National Socialist Freedom Movement. Its organizers included Alfred Rosenberg, the self-proclaimed philosopher of National Socialism. With the aid of General Ludendorff, Rosenberg's group

Alfred Rosenberg was one of the organizers of the National Socialist Freedom Movement. Hitler thought that the success of this group threatened his authority.

entered candidates in the national elections of May 1925.

Thirty-four members of the National Socialist Freedom Movement ran for office. Thirty-two of them were elected. The successful candidates included General Ludendorff, Ernst Röhm, and a National Socialist organizer from Berlin named Gregor Strasser.

Adolf Hitler did not welcome this success. Though it brought National Socialism into the political mainstream, the success threatened his authority. That was a price the Führer was not willing to pay.

Yet another threat to his leadership came from a group centered around his old comrade, Anton Drexler. Drexler saw a chance to get even for past betrayals. He told anyone who would listen that Hitler had "[plotted] against me and broke all his promises, pushed me out, and now has wrecked the party for all time with this crazy Putsch!"[2] Such a man would destroy the Nazi party if his power were not limited, Drexler said.

With all this opposition, even some Hitler loyalists wondered if their Führer could regain his former power. On February 27, 1925, he put their minds at rest. That night, he went back to the scene of the putsch to make his formal return to public life.

He was scheduled to speak at eight

o'clock, but people began arriving in the afternoon. The hall was so crowded that more than a thousand people had to be turned away.

Inside the beer hall, there was barely room to stand. Four thousand people waited to hear Hitler. He spoke to them of party unity. He called upon all National Socialists to "join together behind the swastika flag and crush their two greatest enemies: [Communists] and Jews."[3]

By the time he finished speaking, the crowd was in a frenzy. People shouted "Heil (hail) Hitler!" The word *heil*/hail refers to the act of greeting or acclaiming. The "Hitler salute" was not limited to rallies where the Führer appeared. It became part of everyday life. All over Germany and the occupied nations, loyal Nazis said hello and goodbye with a raised right hand and a hearty "Heil Hitler."

Fighting for Control

Hitler's successful return to public life did not suit the Bavarian government. They banned the Nazi leader from speaking in public for two years. Bans in other German states soon followed. Gone were the giant rallies, the cheering crowds. Without them, Hitler could not hope to reach great masses of

On February 27, 1925, Hitler spoke to thousands of people gathered at the beer hall. He spoke of party unity and crushing their enemies.

people. However, even the loss of his most powerful tool did not stop him.

During the ban, Hitler traveled across Bavaria, holding meetings with small groups of National Socialist Freedom Movement party members. He left the northern wing of the party in the hands of brothers Gregor and Otto Strasser in Berlin.

Hitler did not like placing so much confidence in the Strassers, but he had no choice. Besides dealing with the ban, he had his hands full in Munich. His old friend and comrade Ernst Röhm was getting big ideas.

The Frontbann had been such a success that Röhm wanted to enlarge it. He dreamed of a vast private army, with himself in absolute control. To Hitler, that was unthinkable. He could not allow Röhm, or anyone else, to have such power.

The two leaders quarreled and, as usual, Hitler prevailed. Rather than accept a lesser role, Röhm quit the party and retired from politics. Hitler left the Frontbann to fend for itself. He had other matters on his mind, such as handling the Strasser brothers.

The Problem in Berlin

The Strassers' views on what the party should become did not match Hitler's. They wanted to organize workers against big business. For

Support for Hitler and the Nazi party became a part of everyday life for the German people. Loyal Nazis could be found throughout the country.

Hitler, this was too close to communist beliefs. He wanted to build a master race, not a nation of workers.

Hitler went to Berlin to deal with the problem personally. There, he met a man who would become one of the most important leaders in the Nazi empire. Joseph Goebbels did not fit the Nazi image at all. He was barely five feet tall, with dark eyes and olive skin. Childhood polio had left him with a crippled left foot and a noticeable limp.

During Hitler's time in Berlin, he won Goebbels to his side. In the long run, he was not as successful with the Strassers. However, he was able to silence them for a time with an appeal for party unity. This worked in part because the brothers were divided between themselves. Otto believed that Hitler was a danger to the party and to

the German nation as a whole. Gregor considered him a figurehead who could be controlled. He was not the first, nor the last, person to make that mistake.

Joseph Goebbels did not fit the Nazi image of the physical ideal, but he became valuable to Hitler.

Hitler liked to make a grand entrance into a huge crowd of people to give his speeches.

After settling the problem in Berlin, Hitler returned to Munich. On March 5, 1927, the Bavarian government lifted its public-speaking ban against him. The Führer promptly staged a mass meeting, complete with banners, music, marching troops, and a grand entrance.

Once more, Adolf Hitler had made a political comeback. This time, he would not make the mistake of starting a revolution he could not finish. This time, he had a plan. He would take over Germany without firing a shot or breaking a law.

4

The Road
to Power

In the late 1920s, a "new" Adolf Hitler spoke to the German nation. In public, he appeared more reasonable and statesmanlike. People who had once dismissed him as a hopeless rabble-rouser began listening to what he had to say.

Even with Hitler's new approach, the Nazi party did not control German politics. In fact, the democratic government seemed to be gaining ground. Germany was recovering from its postwar slump.

Hitler knew he needed a national disaster in order to grab power. People did not listen to revolutionaries when times were good. They listened when times were bad, and the nation needed someone to lead it from the brink of disaster.

Hitler and the Great Depression

From Hitler's point of view, the American stock market crash of October, 1929, was a gift from the gods. Almost overnight, rich people lost their fortunes and ordinary people, their life savings. As the American crisis grew, it affected economies all over the world.

In Germany, thousands were thrown out of work. Hopes for prosperity vanished. Communist activity increased, to the great fear of the average German in the middle class. Hitler played the situation with a sure hand. A vast conspiracy of Communists and Jews was responsible for Germany's woes, he said. Unless someone stopped them, they would destroy the German Fatherland.

In speeches all over Germany, Hitler presented himself as that someone. People who had mocked him before began to listen. Nazi party membership grew. So did Nazi presence in the German government. In the election of 1930, Nazi representation in the *Reichstag*, or parliament, shot up from 12 seats to 107.

The Brownshirt Problem

Hitler's new image as "savior" of the Fatherland may have appealed to the German middle class, but it did not appeal to the SA. After the ban on the Nazi party was lifted, the

Brownshirts had come back in force. They were still street brawlers at heart. To them, Hitler's campaigning was a sign of weakness.

The SA's new leader was Franz Pfeffer von Salomon, who had replaced the retired Ernst Röhm. Salomon wanted the SA to become a powerful army in its own right. "The SA man is the sacred freedom fighter," he once wrote. "They are out for all or nothing. They know only the motto . . . Strike dead! You or me!"[1]

Hitler wanted the SA to be more disciplined. He wanted it placed under his personal control. Eventually, Salomon resigned as a result of his disagreements with Hitler.

In desperation, Hitler recalled Röhm from retirement. The Führer named his old comrade to head the SA again. He promised not to interfere in SA matters. In return, he expected the SA to swear an oath of allegiance to him.

Röhm agreed to these terms. Within nine months, he had increased SA membership to 170,000 men. Many members were not former soldiers, but criminals with a violent past. Also many of Röhm's top lieutenants were homosexuals, as was Röhm himself.

For the moment, Hitler generally ignored the criminals and defended the homosexuals. In the Nazi movement, he said, "a man's private life can be an object of consideration

Röhm increased SA membership to 170,000 men. Here, a crowd of SA troops gather.

only if it runs counter to [important] principles of National Socialist [doctrine]."[2]

Under Röhm, the Brownshirts became terrorists, crushing anyone who opposed the Party or its Führer. SA units harassed Jews, Communists, and anyone else whose loyalty to Nazism was questionable.

Because the SA was not officially an arm of the Nazi party, Hitler did not have to take responsibility for its actions. While the Brownshirts cracked heads, he could continue passing himself off as a statesman. As he gained confidence in the political arena,

SA soldiers harassed Jews. Here, a soldier cuts off the beard of a Jewish man.

he moved more surely toward his goal of gaining absolute power.

Hitler Runs for President

In 1932, the former corporal from Austria ran for president of Germany. Hitler's opponent was the current president, Paul von Hindenburg. The aristocratic Hindenburg held the rank of field marshal, highest in the German military. As commander of the army during World War I, he had become a living legend. He first won the presidency in 1925, at the age of seventy-eight.

Hindenburg ran again in 1932, at the advanced age of eighty-five. His only real opposition in that election was Adolf Hitler. Hitler did not run for president because he wanted the office, or even because he thought he could win. He ran because the Nazi party needed a candidate, and he needed the stage a national election would give him.

He did not win the election. However, he did force a runoff—a vote to choose between the two candidates. In that second election, he won 36.1 percent of the vote. That was a good showing against a national hero. It served notice to the German public that Hitler and the Nazis had come to stay. It also paved the way for Hitler's real goal of becoming chancellor of Germany.

Hitler ran against Paul von Hindenburg, left, for the German presidency in 1932.

Hitler's Gamble

In a parliamentary government, the chancellor, or chief of state, is appointed by the president. His first task is to put together a governing majority in the parliament, or legislature. In a system with several political parties, that is often a difficult thing to do. The chancellor must convince two or more parties to work together. If he fails, the president can dissolve the parliament and call for new elections.

This happened twice during 1932. In the first election that July, the Nazis won 230 of approximately 550 seats in the Reichstag. The second election was held in November. But four months had made a big difference in public attitudes. The German people had grown impatient with their stumbling economy. They voted many representatives out of office.

The Nazis lost thirty-four Reichstag seats in the November election. This was a hard blow. The two election campaigns had left the party nearly broke. Some members quit after this reversal of fortune. Others simply stopped paying their party dues.

In such a crisis, most politicians would become cautious. Adolf Hitler did not. He openly sought the chancellorship. To get it, he used the same tactics that had once swept Anton Drexler and others out of his way.

Hitler made an all-or-nothing gamble. He would become chancellor in return for Nazi cooperation in a new government. He flatly refused any lesser position. Some of Hitler's closest advisors disagreed with this tactic. They wanted him to consider a cabinet minister's post or some other important position. Either would give the Nazis a good foundation in national politics. The rest could come later.

The Führer considered this approach timid and unworthy. He held firm: the chancellorship or nothing. The situation looked hopeless for the Nazis until help came from an unexpected source.

Former Chancellor Franz von Papen threw his support behind Adolf Hitler. Papen himself had been unable to form a government by uniting the nationalist, anti-democratic parties. He believed

Franz von Papen supported Adolf Hitler's attempts to become chancellor. He convinced President von Hindenburg to agree to it.

that the Nazi leader could succeed where he had failed.

The chief obstacle to a Hitler chancellorship was President von Hindenburg. The old field marshal disliked the man he privately called "the corporal." As one historian explained, "Neither Hindenburg's conscience nor his duties to the state would . . . permit [him] to turn over power to a Nazi movement that [would use] it for partisan purposes."[3]

Papen set out to change the elderly president's mind. Hitler could be controlled, he said. Papen himself would become vice-chancellor. He would run the government while "the corporal" became little more than a figurehead, a front man without real power. On these terms, the president finally agreed.

The Power-Grab

On January 30, 1933, Adolf Hitler became chancellor of Germany. As he had vowed after his release from Landsberg Prison, he came to power legally. Not a shot was fired; not a law was broken.

The new chancellor soon proved that he would not be just a figurehead. He also proved that even the second highest position in the government would not satisfy him. With each step along the road to power, Adolf Hitler wanted more.

Hitler salutes his followers at a rally soon after his appointment as chancellor.

He moved quickly to get it. As one historian noted, the German public was confused "by the breakneck speed at which, one after another, opponents' positions were captured, leaving them no time to gather and regroup. . . . Hitler later stated that it was his intention to 'seize power swiftly and at one blow.'"[4] Hitler laid the foundation for that blow with cunning and care.

Hitler knew that the best way to unify people is to give them a common enemy. He was able to do this with the help of Hermann Göring and Joseph Goebbels. And communists were the enemy of choice.

On the day after Hitler became Chancellor, he held a conference with Göring and Goebbels. An entry in Goebbels' diary makes the subject of that meeting clear:

> In a conference with the leader we arrange measures for combating the Red [a nickname for communists] terror. For the present we shall [not take] direct action. First the [Communist] attempt at a revolution must burst into flame. At the given moment, we shall strike.[5]

The "Communist Menace"

"Burst into flame" turned out to be more than a figure of speech. On February 27, 1933, fire broke out in the Reichstag building. Communist sympathizer Marinus van der

Fire broke out in the Reichstag building on February 27, 1933. Marinus van der Lubbe was arrested, but the fire was likely the work of the SA.

Lubbe was arrested at the scene. He had a history of mental problems and a police record for starting fires in public buildings around Berlin.

Van der Lubbe may have set a small blaze, but the main fire was almost certainly the work of the SA. Historians are not quite sure how van der Lubbe became involved. Most likely, the Nazis tricked him into starting a fire. At any rate, he was on hand to take the blame.

The Nazis claimed that this was the beginning of a Communist attempt to overthrow the lawful government of Germany. Hitler convinced Hindenburg that the danger was real. On the day after the fire, the president signed an emergency decree, or order. It suspended individual rights such as freedom of speech and assembly, and allowed police to make searches without warrants. It gave the chancellor broad powers to act against enemies of the state.

The Nazis continued to whip up public hysteria about the "Red Menace." They hoped to turn those fears into a landslide victory in the next Reichstag election. They did not, however, entirely achieve that goal.

The Nazis and their allies won a small majority of seats in the Reichstag, but not the sweeping victory they wanted. In what was to be the last free election until after World

War II, the Germans gave the Nazis 44 percent of the vote.

The Law According to Adolf Hitler

Despite this disappointment, Hitler moved ahead with the next step in his climb to power. His plan was to get the Reichstag to give him its power to make laws. To do this, he once more used the threat of a Communist takeover. The Reds were planning to take over Germany, he said. In order to stop them, he needed the power to move quickly. The Enabling Law, as it was called, would give him that power.

This law involved changing the German constitution. It required the support of a two-thirds majority in the Reichstag. When the Nazis could not put together enough votes to get that majority, Hitler fell back on an old habit. He played the statesman while the SA behaved like street rowdies.

On the day the Reichstag was supposed to vote on the Enabling Law, the SA turned out in force. They prevented Communist delegates from entering the Reichstag to vote. Hitler gained the majority he needed.

The Enabling Law gave Hitler powers as a dictator. He could make new laws without consulting the Reichstag or the President. He

When the Reichstag passed the Enabling Law, Hitler was given the powers of a dictator.

could even violate the constitution if he thought it was necessary.

Hitler moved swiftly to consolidate his position. One of his first acts was to order a nationwide boycott of Jewish businesses for April 1. People would not do business with Jews on this day. He followed this with a law that excluded Jews from all government jobs.

On July 14, 1933, he proclaimed the Nazi party the only legal political party in Germany. All others either disbanded voluntarily or were shut down by the SA.

There were only two things left in Hitler's way: President Hindenburg and the Army High Command. The old field marshal was already fading. Hitler was content to play a waiting game with him. He could not do the same with the army, though. He would need the support of the High Command to build a solid base of power. In order to get that support he would have to control Ernst Röhm and the SA.

The Night of Long Knives

It was becoming clear that Röhm had outlived his usefulness. By 1933, the SA had more than two million members. It was a danger to the regular army and also the Nazi party. To make matters worse, Röhm became involved in a homosexual scandal that made

Hitler ordered a nationwide boycott of Jewish businesses on April 1, 1933. SA soldiers block the entrance to a Jewish-owned store.

the front page of the Munich newspaper. The Führer made a great show of being shocked to discover that the SA harbored homosexuals and violent criminals.

Something had to be done, he said. He called on Heinrich Himmler and Hermann Göring to handle the problem. By this time, Himmler had built the SS into a disciplined and fanatical force loyal to Hitler. Göring had formed the *Gestapo*, an equally fearsome secret police unit in the German state of Prussia.

On June 30, 1934, the SS and Gestapo began a purge of the SA. It came to be known as "the Night of Long Knives," though the killing lasted for more than three days. Dozens of Brownshirts and others suspected of disloyalty were imprisoned or killed outright. Others, including Röhm himself, were arrested and later executed.

According to reports from witnesses, the SS executioners gave Röhm a loaded gun. This was to allow him the "honorable" alternative of suicide. Röhm did not use the gun. "If I am to be killed, let Adolf do it himself," he said.[6] Then he stood at attention until the executioners shot him dead.

Among the victims of the Night of Long Knives was Hitler's rival Gregor Strasser. The man who had wanted a truly socialist state was gunned down in his jail cell. His killers stood outside and fired through the window while Strasser "dodged around like a rat in a cage until wounded."[7] Otto Strasser managed to escape his brother's fate. He left the country and eventually found his way to Canada.

The Night of Long Knives changed the Nazi party. The SA was in shambles and its leaders were dead. Hitler was finally able to win army support. All he had to do now was wait until the ailing Hindenburg was out of the way.

5

Building the Third Reich

President Paul von Hindenburg died on August 2, 1934. At a large public funeral, Adolf Hitler paid tribute to him. Then he promptly combined the offices of president and chancellor and proclaimed himself Supreme Leader of the German Nation.

Now Hitler could move ahead even more rapidly than before. He did what he had always said he would do: made Germany into a police state and Nazism into a way of life. On this foundation, he planned to build the Aryan master race and conquer new territory for German settlement.

The Nazification of Germany

The SS played a major role in making Germany into a Nazi state. Under the sinister

Heinrich Himmler, the SS had become a vast monster. Many parts had overlapping authority. Criminal police dealt with ordinary crimes, such as burglary and assault. State security police dealt with racial issues, ensured loyalty to the Führer, and punished those who would not go along. Even Hermann Göring's Gestapo became part of the SS.

The SS and the Gestapo turned Germany into a brutal National Socialist society. There was National Socialist education, law,

The SS and Gestapo, shown here, were brutal in their enforcement of Nazism.

medicine, commerce, and industry. There was even National Socialist recreation and entertainment.

Schools taught "racial science" to six-year-olds, and reverence for the Führer along with reverence for God. In the city of Cologne, for example, children in the party-sponsored lunch program repeated the following blessing before eating:

> Führer, my Führer, [given] to me by the Lord,
> Protect and preserve me as long as I live!
> [You have] rescued Germany from deepest distress,
> I thank [you] today for my daily bread.
> [Abide] long with me, [forsake] me not,
> Führer, my Führer, my faith and my light!
> Heil, mein Führer![1]

All loyal Germans were expected to belong to one or more Nazi groups. Young people joined the Hitler Youth. Adults had a dizzying variety of professional associations, sports clubs, and social groups. Membership in these groups was not voluntary. Everybody had to belong and everybody had to attend. Those who did not could expect an unpleasant visit from the SS or Gestapo.

Most importantly, every German was expected to show proper reverence for the Führer. Criticism was not allowed. Neither was joking at the Führer's expense. Hitler

Loyal Germans were expected to belong to at least one Nazi group. Young people joined the Hitler Youth.

became a godlike figure, apart from even his closest associates.

In this cold Nazi world, simply forgetting the proper greeting could cause trouble. As writer Ilse-Margret Vogel recalled, "In Görlitz, my hometown, one became suspect—and could even be denounced and arrested—for not using the required Hitler greeting: raising the right arm and saying, 'Heil, Hitler.'"[2]

The Myth of a Master Race

In addition to a proper attitude toward National Socialism, Germans were expected

The salute shown here was required of all Germans. People could be arrested if they did not raise their right arms and say "Heil, Hitler."

to be conscious of race. Only people of German and Northern European heritage were to be part of the Nazi future. Jews, people of color, and other non-Aryans did not belong. Their very blood was thought to be polluted, or dirty.

Even full Aryans were not entirely safe from Nazi racial policies. One of the earliest laws was aimed at Germans with genetic, or inherited, diseases. The Law for the Prevention of Genetically Diseased Offspring became official on July 14, 1933. It allowed forced sterilization of people with hereditary diseases. By preventing these people from having children, the Nazis hoped to improve the so-called Aryan race.

On the other side of the coin, the Nazis called upon genetically healthy Aryans to produce as many children as possible. The responsibility for this fell chiefly upon women. German women were told to bear children early and often. They were told that this was the purpose of their existence.

Controlling reproduction was an important part of the Nazi racial hygiene movement.[3] The word hygiene simply means the promotion and preservation of health. There is nothing sinister, or evil, about it. Racial hygiene is another matter. The Nazis used it to serve their notion of a German master race.

People with hereditary diseases and disabilities were prevented from having children.

In the name of racial hygiene, the Nazis prohibited intermarriage between Aryans and non-Aryans. An Aryan who married or partnered with a Jew or person of color was a race criminal and could go to prison. Children of these unions were mongrels.

In time, the myth of the master race would take Germany beyond controlling who had children and who did not. It would be used to justify the killing of "defective" babies and mentally retarded or mentally ill children and adults. It would furnish a reason for genocide, the systematic killing of entire peoples.

The Quest for Lebensraum

Nazi racial policies were linked to plans for expanding German territory. Hitler wanted lebensraum, or living space, for all those large, Aryan families. He intended to get it by any means necessary, including war.

Before he could carry out his plan for German expansion, Hitler had to rebuild the military, a process called rearmament. To do that, he would have to violate the Treaty of Versailles. He did not renounce the treaty or formally declare his intentions to rearm. He simply started building Germany's military strength, all the while declaring his peaceful intentions.

Rearmament had an immediate effect on the German economy. It created jobs and new prosperity. The Führer's popularity soared. According to historian John Weiss, this prosperity was only a byproduct of Hitler's true purpose. "When the arms were used," he wrote,

> the twin 'final solutions,' lebensraum and genocide, would bring a permanent solution. United, armed, and free of their mortal enemy, the Jews, Nordic Germany would prosper. The war in the east and the Holocaust were [always] connected in the Nazi [mind].[4]

By invading eastern Europe and then Russia, the Nazis planned to create living space for Germans by slaughtering huge numbers of "racially inferior" people and taking their lands.

On March 16, 1935, Germany began drafting young men into the armed services. The army grew well beyond the limit of 100,000 men set by the Treaty of Versailles. Still, Hitler continued to proclaim his peaceful intentions. He did not believe that other countries would risk a confrontation over a technical violation of the treaty. He was correct. The nations of Europe did not respond.

A year later, the new German army marched into the Rhineland. Allied troops had barred Germany from this strip of land along the Rhine River after World War I. But by 1930, the last of the Allied troops were gone, and the area was demilitarized.

Hitler was quick to point out that his march into the Rhineland was not an invasion. The troops entered peacefully. No shots were fired, no blood was spilled. The army was simply protecting the interests of Rhineland Germans.

With each step, Hitler grew bolder. In March, 1938, Germany took over Austria. This *anschluss*, or annexation, took place without war. This was partly because a majority of Austrians favored union with Germany. Hitler browbeat and threatened Austrian leaders into holding a special election, confident that the people would vote as he wished. They did, overwhelmingly approving the annexation.

Next, Hitler took territory from Czechoslovakia. First came the Sudentenland, a region along the Czech-German border. Once again, there was no bloodshed. Hitler took the Sudentenland by diplomatic agreement.

The Munich Agreement, as it came to be called, was signed on September 30, 1938. In exchange for Hitler's pledge that the Sudentenland would be his "last territorial demand," England, France, and Italy agreed not to interfere.[5] The Czechs, who actually lost the territory, had no say in the matter.

Just six months later, Hitler violated his

Hitler annexed Austria in March of 1938. This sign reads
"75 million yes! One people, one empire, one führer."

promise. In March, 1939, Germany took the rest of Czechoslovakia. Once again, there was no bloodshed. The Nazis intimidated the Czech leadership and maneuvered them into accepting the new order. England and the other Versailles powers did nothing.

The European nations continued to hope that this policy of appeasement, or giving Hitler what he wanted, would prevent war. At each step along the way, Hitler justified his actions and made new promises— promises he did not intend to keep.

The Road to War

When Hitler began making demands on Poland in 1939, England and France stepped in to guarantee Polish borders. Before crossing that line, Hitler made sure the Soviet Union would not oppose him. On August 23, 1939, he and Soviet dictator Josef Stalin made a non-aggression pact, an agreement that the nations would not fight one another.

On September 1, Nazi troops invaded Poland. Britain and France promptly declared war on Germany. Hitler adviser Albert Speer later recalled that the Führer was genuinely surprised. He had expected the British and French to back down as they had done before.

According to Speer, Hitler

> quickly reassured himself . . . that England and France had . . . declared war merely as a sham,

Nazi troops invaded Poland in September, 1939. German troops marched through Warsaw.

in order not to lose face before the whole world. . . . He [believed] that the West was too feeble, too worn out, and too [soft] to begin the war seriously. Probably, it was . . . embarrassing for him to admit . . . that he had made so crucial a mistake."[6]

It was the same kind of mistake Hitler had made in the Beer Hall Putsch, sixteen years earlier. He had extended himself too far. In 1923, his misjudgment created a brief disturbance in Munich. In 1939, it launched one of the darkest chapters in human history.

From the beginning, World War II was different from other wars. Hitler had two goals: to gain lebensraum for the German people and to build a racial state. England and its allies had one goal: to stop the spread of Nazism through Europe and the world. It was not only about preventing Hitler from building

his empire and gaining lebensraum for the German people. It was also about preventing the Nazis from building a racial state.

Albert Speer was one of Hitler's advisers. According to Speer, Hitler was surprised when the British and French declared war.

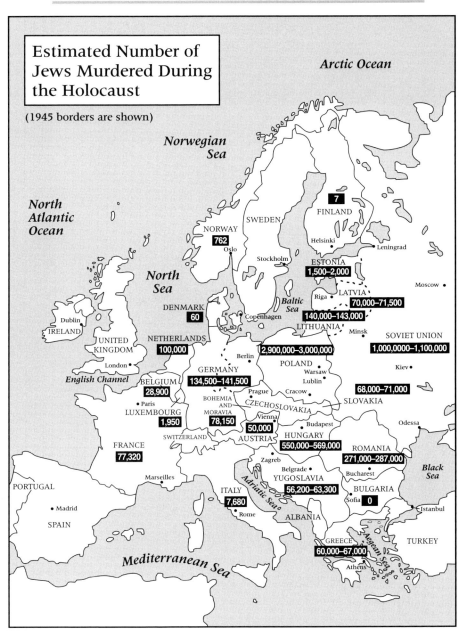

Estimated Number of Jews Murdered During the Holocaust

(1945 borders are shown)

Arctic Ocean

Norwegian Sea

North Atlantic Ocean

FINLAND **7**

Helsinki

Leningrad

NORWAY **762**

Oslo

SWEDEN

Stockholm

ESTONIA **1,500–2,000**

Moscow

North Sea

Baltic Sea

Riga

LATVIA **70,000–71,500**

DENMARK **60**

Copenhagen

LITHUANIA

Minsk

SOVIET UNION **1,000,0000–1,100,000**

Dublin

IRELAND

UNITED KINGDOM

NETHERLANDS **100,000**

Berlin

POLAND

Warsaw

Kiev

London

English Channel

GERMANY **134,500–141,500**

Lublin

BELGIUM **28,900**

Paris

LUXEMBOURG **1,950**

BOHEMIA AND MORAVIA **78,150**

Prague

Cracow

CZECHOSLOVAKIA

SLOVAKIA **68,000–71,000**

Vienna

Budapest

Odessa

FRANCE **77,320**

SWITZERLAND

AUSTRIA **50,000**

HUNGARY **550,000–569,000**

ROMANIA **271,000–287,000**

Zagreb

Belgrade

Bucharest

Black Sea

Marseilles

YUGOSLAVIA **56,200–63,300**

BULGARIA **0**

Sofia

PORTUGAL

ITALY **7,680**

Rome

Adriatic Sea

ALBANIA

Istanbul

Madrid

SPAIN

GREECE **60,000–67,000**

Athens

Aegean Sea

TURKEY

Mediterranean Sea

This map shows the estimated numbers of Jews killed in each European country during the Holocaust. Approximately 11 million people, 6 million of them Jews, were killed during the Holocaust.

Hitler's first goal led to the battlefield. His second led to death camps and gas chambers. Together, these goals would claim some 55 million human lives and involve sixty countries in war. In the process, they would leave a legacy of hatred that humankind would never forget.

Timeline

November 11, 1918—End of World War I. Germany surrenders.

June 28, 1919—Treaty of Versailles signed. Germany forced to accept strict terms.

September 12, 1919—Adolf Hitler attends his first meeting of the German Workers Party.

April 1, 1920—German Workers Party becomes the National Socialist German Workers (Nazi) Party.

November 8, 1923—Beer Hall Putsch takes place.

April 1, 1924—Hitler sentenced to five years in prison for the putsch.

December 20, 1924—Hitler released from Landsberg Prison after serving less than nine months of his sentence.

February 27, 1925—Bavarian government bans Hitler from public speaking.

April 1925—Ernst Röhm withdraws from public life. Hitler creates the SS.

March 5, 1927—Bavarian government lifts the speaking ban on Adolf Hitler.

January 30, 1933—Hitler sworn in as chancellor of Germany.

February 27, 1933—Reichstag fire occurs.

February 28, 1933—Presidential decree grants Hitler emergency powers.

March 5, 1933—Reichstag elections. Nazis and their nationalist allies win a slim majority.

March 24, 1933—Reichstag passes the Enabling Law, giving Hitler dictatorial powers.

December 1, 1933—Nazi party is made the only lawful party in Germany.

June 30, 1934—The "Night of Long Knives" begins. Ernst Röhm and others executed.

August 2, 1934—Death of President Hindenburg. Hitler declares himself absolute ruler of the German nation.

March 16, 1935—Germany begins drafting men into military service.

March 7, 1936—German troops enter the Rhineland in violation of the Treaty of Versailles.

March 13, 1938—Anschluss. Germany annexes Austria.

September 29, 1938—Munich Agreement surrenders the Sudentenland to Germany.

March 19, 1939—Germany takes control of the rest of Czechoslovakia.

August 23, 1939—Germany signs a non-aggression pact with the Soviet Union.

September 1, 1939—Germany invades Poland. World War II begins.

Chapter Notes

Chapter 1. Beginnings

1. Margot Stern Strom and William S. Parsons, *Facing History and Ourselves: Holocaust and Human Behavior* (Watertown, Mass.: Intentional Educations, Inc., 1982), p. 73.

2. John Toland, *Adolf Hitler* (New York: Doubleday, 1976), p. 5.

3. Adolf Hitler, Ralph Manheim, trans., *Mein Kampf* (Boston: Houghton Mifflin, 1971), p. 123.

4. Toland, p. 84.

5. Alan Bullock, *Hitler: A Study in Tyranny*, revised ed. (New York: Bantam, 1961), p. 41.

Chapter 2. The Growth of National Socialism

1. Richard Thurlow, *Fascism* (Cambridge, England: Cambridge University Press, 1999), p. 1.

2. George L. Mosse, *Nazi Culture: A Documentary History* (New York: Schocken Books, 1981), p. 102.

3. William L. Shirer, *The Rise and Fall of the Third Reich* (New York: Fawcett Publications, 1962), p. 74.

4. Joachim E. Fest, *The Face of the Third Reich: Portraits of the Nazi Leadership* (New York: Da Capo Press, 1999), p. 72.

5. Shirer, p. 123.

6. Ibid.

Chapter 3. A Failed Revolution

1. Konrad Heiden, Ralph Manheim, trans., *Der Fuehrer: Hitler's Rise to Power* (Boston: Beacon Press, 1969), p. 190.

2. John Toland, *Adolf Hitler* (New York: Doubleday, 1976), p. 196.

3. Ibid., p. 207.

Chapter 4. The Road to Power

1. Joachim E. Fest, *The Face of the Third Reich: Portraits of the Nazi Leadership* (New York: Da Capo Press, 1999), pp. 142-143.

2. Ibid., p. 144.

3. Henry Ashby Turner, Jr., *Hitler's Thirty Days to Power* (Reading, Mass.: Addison-Wesley Publishing Co., 1996), p. 12.

4. Fest, p. 42.

5. Alan Bullock, *Hitler: A Study in Tyranny*, revised ed. (New York: Bantam, 1961), p. 221.

6. William L. Shirer, *The Rise and Fall of the Third Reich* (New York: Fawcett Publications, 1962), p. 308.

7. John Toland, *Adolf Hitler* (New York: Doubleday, 1976), p. 345.

Chapter 5. Building the Third Reich

1. George L. Mosse, *Nazi Culture: A Documentary History* (New York: Schocken Books, 1981), p. 241.

2. Ilse-Margret Vogel, *Bad Times, Good Friends: A Personal Memoir* (New York: Harcourt Brace Jovanovich Publishers, 1992), p. x.

3. Robert N. Proctor, *Racial Hygiene: Medicine Under the Nazis* (Cambridge, Mass.: Harvard University Press, 1988), p. 124.

4. John Weiss, *Ideology of Death: Why the Holocaust Happened in Germany* (Chicago: Ivan R. Dee, 1996), pp. 317–318.

5. Ian Kershaw, *Hitler: 1936–1945 Nemesis* (New York: W.W. Norton and Company, 2000), p. 173.

6. Albert Speer, Richard and Clara Winston, trans., *Inside the Third Reich: Memoirs by Albert Speer* (New York: Galahad Books, 1995), p. 165.

Glossary

Allies—During World War II, the group of nations headed by Great Britain and later joined by the United States and the Soviet Union.

anti-Semitism—Hatred of, or discrimination against, Jews as a group.

Aryan—Nazi term for Nordic, or Northern European, peoples.

Axis—During World War II, the group of nations headed by Germany and opposing the Allies.

chancellor—Head of State in a parliamentary government.

communism—A form of government in which property is communally owned.

decree—A formal and authoritative order.

fascism—A one-party system of government in which society is controlled by military force, secret police, and censorship.

Final Solution—The term applied to Nazi plans to exterminate the Jewish people.

genetics—The science dealing with inherited characteristics of life forms.

genocide—The systematic extermination, or attempted extermination, of an entire racial, ethnic, political, or religious group.

German Workers' Party—The political party that became the foundation of the Nazi party.

Gestapo *(Geheime-Staats-Polizei)*—A secret state police agency in Nazi Germany.

Holocaust—Originally, an all-consuming fire. Used to describe the extermination of more than eleven million people, including six million Jews.

leadership principle—The idea that complete authority rests with one person, or one small group.

lebensraum (living space)—Nazi term for expansion of German territory.

master race—Nazi term for Germanic peoples who were regarded as superior to all other races.

Nazi party—National Socialist German Workers Party. The party of Adolf Hitler.

platform—In politics, a statement of basic principles.

police state—A government in which the will of a dictatorial regime is enforced by police agencies possessing broad powers.

propaganda—A presentation of ideas slanted to shape and control public opinion.

putsch—An uprising or rebellion from within.

rabble-rouser—A person with the ability to sway masses of people in a particular direction.

racial hygiene—The idea of protecting the genetic health of a people through selective breeding and other measures.

racism—An irrational belief in the superiority of a given group, based upon inborn racial traits.

Reichstag—the German parliament, or legislative body.

SA *(Sturmabteilung)*—"storm troops." In the early days of the Nazi party, a private army used to intimidate and control enemies. Often called "Brownshirts" after the color of their uniforms.

SS *(Shutzstaffel)*—"protection squad." The elite guard of the Nazi state. It administered the Final Solution and insured obedience to the dictates of the Führer.

sterilize—To deprive of the ability to produce offspring.

swastika—The hooked cross symbol of the Nazi party.

Thousand Year Reich—Hitler's name for the empire that he vowed would last a thousand years.

Treaty of Versailles—The formal agreement that ended World War I.

warrant—A legal order permitting arrest, search, or seizure of property.

Further Reading and Internet Addresses

Ayer, Eleanor H., Helen Waterford, and Alfons Heck. *Parallel Journeys*. New York: Aladdin Paperbacks, 2000.

Heyes, Eileen. *Adolf Hitler*. Brookfield, CT: Millbrook Press, 1994.

Marrin, Albert. *Hitler*. New York: Penguin Putnam Books for Young Readers, 1993.

Tames, Richard. *Fascism*. Chicago, IL: Raintree Publishers, 2002.

Vogel, Ilse-Margret. *Bad Times, Good Friends: A Memoir—Berlin 1945*. San Diego: Harcourt Brace Jovanovich, 1992.

Internet Addresses

Simon Wiesenthal Center: Multimedia Learning Center
http://motlc.wiesenthal.org/index.html

United States Holocaust Memorial Museum
http://www.ushmm.org

Index